I0148648

T. R. (Thomas Robinson) Dawley

The President Lincoln Campaign Songster

T. R. (Thomas Robinson) Dawley

The President Lincoln Campaign Songster

ISBN/EAN: 9783743323469

Manufactured in Europe, USA, Canada, Australia, Japa

Cover: Foto ©ninafisch / pixelio.de

Manufactured and distributed by brebook publishing software
(www.brebook.com)

T. R. (Thomas Robinson) Dawley

The President Lincoln Campaign Songster

THE

PRESIDENT

LINCOLN

CAMPAIGN

SONGSTER.

NEW YORK:

T. R. DAWLEY. Publisher for the Million.

13 AND 15 PARK ROW.

CONTENTS.

THE

PRESIDENT LINCOLN

SONGSTER.

——‡o‡——

TO OUR PRESIDENT

Suggested by his " Patriotic Stockings."

O, thou who through these bloody years
  Has passed the flame, untainted,
And while strong hearts grow weak with fears,
  Has faltered not, nor fainted,—
While Southtons sneer and traitors hoot,
  And myriad meshes bound thee,
Treadest the false flag under foot,
  And winds the true one 'round thee;

Go on, go on, O, honored chief!
  Thy virtue undiminished;
The work begun, 'tis our belief
  Will still be thine till finished,
Let treason perish, branch and root,
  And when our land has crowned thee,
The " bars" shall writhe beneath thy feet,
  The "stars" be twined around thee!

When " parlor" soldiers gather round,
  And flatter for promotion,
Who cannot show a single wound,
  Or battle field's devotion—
Though all their words fall smooth and, sweet.
  Though all their friends should float thee,
Cast the false patriot 'neath thy feet,
  But bind the true about thee.

When friends who knew thee not till Fame
  Had shown thy future glory,
Cringe, suppliant, 'round thine honored name,
  And chant aloud thy story—
Tear off the mask, the gilded suit,
  Through which such false ones woo thee ;
Tread the mock friendship under foot,
  But link the true one to thee.

And O! when all thy work is done
  For this franchised nation—
When thou art nearing, like a Sun,
  The verge of the Creation—
When thou art leaving earth, to meet
  The friends whose love once bound thee,
O, cast all false faith, 'neath thy feet,
  And fold the true around thee!

THE UNION LEAGUE SOLDIERS SONG.
Air :—" *Old Dan Tucker.*"

When this cruel war began,
Slidell he to England ran,
To be recognized he was bent,
The Queen she would not give consent.

Chorus.—So clear the track for vet'ran boys,
    For they are bound to make a noise ;
    Get out of the way you rebels all.
    We'll flog you out before next fall,

Johnny Bull he then did say,
Slidell, you'd better go away;
Oppose the North it will not do,
They'll flog the North and England too.

The Queen she then did speak again,
You'd better with the North remain;
Said Palmerston, and so do I,
If we help you we must be sly

Said Davis I will try again,
Then Russell said it's all in vain;
For Johnny Bull he dare not brag,
For fear that he would die a stag.

Then Yancey said we were a fool
To think king Cotton it would rule;
But the blockade has spoilt our fun,
And I'm afraid we are undone.

We all did think at Bull Run fight,
That we the South had a good sight;
But since that time we've had to learn
That our king Cotton we must burn.

England she has frowned upon us,
And left us in a mighty fuss;
I feel sorry for what we've done.
We lay it all to Buchanan.

We thought that Lincoln was not true,
And that the South he would undo;
Our northern friends they said the same,
And told us we were not to blame.

And now we think that he is just
To North and South to East and West;
And if we could, I think that all
Would vote for him the coming fall,

We thought that Breckenridge and Lee,
And Floyd and Tombs the South would free:
But Jeff, he has deceived us all,
We hope he'll die before next fall.

He told us that the North was small,
And that they could not fight at all;
But you may judge of our surprise,
When we saw them like legions rise!

Then Grant and Mead and Burnside too,
They are bound to put us through;
We are surrounded as you see —
Our doom is sealed eternally.

Think of the places we have lost,
And what Secession rage has cost,
We've lost our homes and negroes too,—
We all begin too feel quite blue.

Come all ye nations far and near,
Never rebel for just look here!
You see starvation and disgrace
Are heaped upon the southern race.

We sound the trumpet, beat the drum,
From Tennessee to Washington;
From Kansas to the State of Maine,
The Copperheads shall never reign,

Chorus.—So clear the track, &c.

LINCOLN, FREEDOM VICTORY.

Air :—" *The American Flag.*"

From Maryland, " My Maryland,"
  That State home of Contention,
A Mr. Harris joined the band
  That met in a convention
To nominate a candidate
To fill the highest chair of State !

But there was something said or done,
  That riled the Marylander ;
His rampauts had no wood-en gun ;
  To parly he'd not pander,
So Mr. Harris rose to say
Just what he thought in his own way.

He did not think that Little Mac
  Was such a hero as they thought him ;
And—then just then he got a crack—
  (Right on the scene the blow it caught him)
For that convention held " Free Speech"
An apple Harris should not reach.

" Down with the man who cries down Mac !"
  " Flatten the 'pin that pricks the bubble ;"
" Lay the base ingrate on his back !"
  " Give him a trashing for his trouble !"
These were the answers Harris heard ;
For Free Speech there was not a word.

" My Maryland, My Maryland."
  Are ye to freedom friend or foeman ?
Where in the battle do you stand ?
  As base born slave, or studdy yeomen ?
If for Free Speech you ask to day,
Come with us who would show the way !

We spike no guns when victories dawn;
  We furl no flags when triumphs wait us;
Our shouts upon the air are borne,
  While they are silent all, who hate us;
Our cry from Lake to Gulf and Sea.
Is, Lincoln! Freedom! Victory!

———

BURIAL OF JOHN C. FREMONT.

AIR:—*Not Yet Found.*

Not a sigh was heard nor a funeral groan,
  As to the Salt River banks we hurried;
But we longed to leave the "corpus" alone,
  And we heartily wished he was buried.

We buried him deep on election day.
  (All our votes for the Union throwing)
And "smiled" as we passed the spot where he lay
  Our regard for the Pathfinder showing.

No plaited linen enclosed his breast,
  But in a wet blanket we wound him;
And he lay like a mustang taking his rest,
  No "body-guard" not "kerridge" around him.

But half of our pleasant task was done,
  When Salt River the moonbeams reflected;
And we knew by the booming of Union guns,
  That Andy and Abe were elected.

Quickly and gladly we laid him down,
  And we made not a sigh of sorrow;
But we thought if we liv'd and got some "old rye,"
  We'd have a good time on the morrow.

THE CAMPAIGN IS OPENED.

AIR:--" *The Battle cry of Freedom.*"

The campaign is opened for Eighteen Sixty-four,
  Our best blood is flowing for freedom ;
Grant has crossed the Rapidan, and we hear the can-
    non's roar,
  'Mid shouts of the brave sons of freedom.
    Huzza! for the Union, huzza! boys, huzza
    Down with the traitors who trample on the law,
    Then rally 'round the flag boys—our fathers did
      of yore—
    Shouting the battle cry of freedom.

General Lee is driven back, with ULYSSUS on the
    track,
  Shouting the battle cry of freedom ;
And old Ricmond's bound to fall, for the " writing's on
    the wall."
  Read it ye gallant sons of freedom.
    Huzza! for the Union, huzza! boys, huzza!

General Grant is a Captain on whom we can rely,
  Shouting the battle cry of freedom ;
He never has been beaten, and will conquer Lee, or
    die,
  Shouting the battle cry of freedom.
    Huzza ! for the Union, huzza ! boys, huzza!

Soon the victory will be ours, and we'll strew with
    brilliant flowers,
  The path of the brave sons of freedom ;
Who 'mid the bloody strife, have perilled limb and
    life,
  In battling for Union, and freedom.
    Huzza! for the Union, huzza! boys, huzza!

THE END IS NIGH.

Yes brave boys, the end is coming ;
　　Soon its shades will appear,
　When the hearts of friends will gladden,
　　They rejoice the end is near.

Though obscured by treason's banner,
　　Which is feebly held on high,
By a band of plotting traitors,
　　Who well knew their end is nigh.

They are failing sadly failing ;
　　From hope's path they're rudely cast,
On destruction's path they're sailing ;
　　Ah, their end is coming fast.

Infamy shall mark here after
　　Where once Treason's banner waved,
Now by Union arms 'tws severed,
　　And the grand Republic saved.

YE COPPERHEADS.

Air :—" The American Boy."

Father, pray, tell what ye Copperhead is,
　　Ye people are talking about ;
And where does he dwell, and what is his form,
　　Is he tall, is he slender or stout ?
Or has he all forms, or is he so named
　　From ye thinness and shape of his brains ?
Or is he so named from his treacherous heart
　　And ye venom and gall it contains ?

Away in ye wild and ye jungle, my son,
  A serpent lies coiled in ye brake,
Though all on ye surface looks smiling and fair,
  Yet under is hidden ye snake ;
Ye innocent foot, as it passeth along,
  Unconscious of enemy near,
Ye treacherous serpent wounds deep with its sting,
  Then sneakingly hideth in fear.

And thus to a country of wide-spreading plain,
  Of cotton, and lonely cane-brake,
Men come from the North with sympathy-spice,
  And feed to ye secession snake ;
When Union and Liberty journey through gloom,
  They wound as ye Copperhead do.
They sneak, and they stab in the dark, and that's
    why
  We call them ye Copperheads too,

RALLY FOR OUR FLAG.

AIR:—" *Araby's Daughter.*"

Like the rock, which in vain the waves madly assail,
You still stand as firmly, for truth must prevail ;
Though traitors most foul would your colors disgrace,
Every star shines still brightly, not one is defaced.

Those who seek to degrade you, their pride will de-
    cay,
Like the foam on the ocean, their might pass away ;
Their grandeur will fade, like a vision from sight,
While still proudly you'll stand, in your triumph and
    might.

Brave men round you rally, to succor and save,
And their bright path of fame often leads to the
　　　grave,
Still your stars and your stripes calmly wave o'er the
　　　sod,
·Where those heroes, who fell, gave their souls to
　　　their God.

Like the clear beacon light, o'er the wild waters
　　　thrown,
That forms a bright path to the mariner's home ;
An emblem of Liberty, faithful you shine,
Surtained by Omnipotent power divine.

Our glorious Union shall rise in her might,
Like gold from the ashes, more raidiant and bright ;
And our country, for aye! become many in one,
While millions proclaim our triumph is won.

HOME TRAITORS.

Air :—"*Immortal Washington.*"

There are foes, here at home,
　　Bad as those in the field,
And they damage our cause day by day;
　　One has shouldered the gun,
　　While the other's concealed,
Like an adder, to spring on his prey.
　　We more easily know
　　Of our foe with the sword,
And his action is plain unto all;
　　But the traitor at home,
　　In the village and ward,
Is a working as hard for our fall.

Chorus—We care not if father,
  Or brother, or friend,
Or, no matter, if bone of our bone,
  While firing our cannon
  At foes in the field,
Let us look at the traitor at home!

  Now the traitor, at home,
  Is a shrewd, wily knave ;
He has talent and friends at command :
  He would fight in the field
  By the rebel so brave,
But a spark in the North must be fanned.
  He's a diplomat, sure,
  For the enemy's soil,
Though a sly, cunning rogue, we confess ;
  He is always about
  'Mong the weaker to toil,
Or to write for the copperhead press.

Chorus—We care not if father,
  Or brother, or friend,
Or, no matter, if bone of our bone,
  While firing our cannon
  At foes in the field,
LET US LOOK TO THE TRAITOR AT HOME!

THE SCOURGED BACK.

  A wilderness of scars !
A field, by tangled furrows torn and riven !
A sea of waves, by meeting whirlwinds driven !
A cloud, storm-shatter'd through the midnight
  Heaven !
  A wreck of rayless stars !

A human form! O God!
Who of one blood hast made all tribes below,
Is this thy work, thy image, mangled so?
Ay; thus was thy Son, for human woe,
    Scourged by the soldiers' rod.

A human form! Oh, yes;
That skin had nerves as exquisite as thine;
That flesh could quiver, like my child's, or mine;
Those muscles writhed, when floods of burning brine
    Drench'd their gash'd nakedness.

Why was it done, or borne?
Behold the brow that crowns that manly form!
See the strong shoulder and the sinewy arm!
'Twas done to crush that *man* into a *worm!*
    'Twas borne in hope of morn.

But all is over now:
A deep sereneness of unearthly grace
Sheds soft o'er every lineament its trace;
Hell's mark behind, but Heaven's on its face,
    And victory on his brow.

The sun, with golden pen,
Has drawn two pictures here, and all may read:
" Curst be the fiends who wrought this devilish
    deed ? "
Nay, rather curse the worse than devilish creed
    That makes such fiends of men.

Send such men back to chains?
Not while a conscious nation feels and thinks!
Not till each freeman's lifted right arm shrinks!
Not till the perjured land that dares it sinks!
    And God no longer reigns!

THE LOYAL LEAGUER'S SONG.

Air: " *The Wedding of Ballyporeen.*"

What nonsense to prate about Freedom and Right ;
He has freedom enough who has freedom to fight ;
So, shoulder your muskets and muzzle your clack,
And a war-charger make of each old party hack
    Then, hurrah for strong vigorous measures !
    Hurrah for strong vigorous measures !
    Hurrah for strong vigorous measures !
    Some good healthy hanging for me !

Down, down with the traitors who clamor for peace ;
Make war upon them and our troubles will cease ;
Or give them an office and peace they'll forego,
For no placemen or peacemen I'd have you to know
    For they go for strong vigorous measures !
    They go for strong vigorous measures !
    They go for strong vigorous measures !
    No peacemen or traitors are they !

Our government's strong and our government's wise,
And, mark me !, 'twill soon take the world by surprise;
For I've telegraphs got, and this way they run—
"Look out ! something somewhere will shortly be done!
    Then hurrah for strong vigorous measures !
    Hurrah for strong vigorous measures !
    Hurrah for strong vigorous measures !
    Some healthy blood letting for me !

OII THEN RALLY BRAVE MEN.

AIR:—" *Battlee Cry of Freedom.*"

When our banner went down, with its anc'ent re-
nown,
Betrayed and degraded by treason,
Did they think, as it fell, what a passion would swell
Our hearts when we asked them the reason?

Chorus—Oh! then rally, brave men, to the standard
again,
The flag that proclaimed us a nation!
We will fight, on its part, while there's life
in a heart.
And then trust to the next generation.

Although causeless the blow that at Sumter laid low
That flag, it was seed for the morrow;
And a thousand flags flew for the one that fell true,
As traitors have found to their sorrow.

Chorus.—Oh! then, rally, brave men, to the standard
again,
The flag that proclaims us a nation!.
We will fight, on its part, while theres life in
a heart.
And then trust to the next generation.

'Twas in flashes of flame it was brought to a shame,
Till then unrecorded in story.
But in the flashes as bright it shall rise in our sight,
And float over Sumter in glory!

Chorus.—Oh! then rally, brave men, to the standard
again,
The flag that proclaimed us a nation!
We'll fight, on its part, while there's life in
a heart.
And then trust to the next generarion.

THE COPPERHEADS FAREWELL TO HIS MAS-TER.

Aɪʀ:—" *The Tune the Old Cow died on.*"

I'm thinking of the time, Jeff., when life was bright
    and fair,
Ere that my soul was steeped in guilt when innocence
    dwelt there,
When I could meet my fellow man with proud and
    lofty mien,
It grieves me to look back, Jeff., its poisonous venom
    shed !"
The deadly potion changed the man into a " Copper-
    head !"

The friends who knew me once, Jeff., they scorn to
    meet me more.
And even those whom I have served, have turned me
    from their door ;
With slimy reptiles now I squirm, within some loath-
    some den.
Hiding our traitorous forms from light, shrinking from
    honest men !
The brand of Cain is on my brow, its course is o'er me
    spread.
The passing breeze e'en seems to say—there goes a
    " Copperhead !"

I've chill'd the manly loyal heart as to the field it
    hied
To battle for the glorious cause for which our fathers
    died
I've paralyzed his upraised arm by falsehood's cun-
    ning ways,
And robbed the martyr of his fame, the hero of his
    praise !

I've learned to smile when freemen died, and loyal
  blood was shed,
And turned and stung them as they fell—just like a
  " Copperhead !"

I've seen mine only son, Jeff., quit his paternal roof
To aid his stricken native land, whilst I stood far
  aloof ;
And as his young life oozed away and stained his
  lowly bed,
I felt a double weight of guilt—his blood was on my
  head !
Yet as his eyelids closed in death, with feeble voice
  he said ;
" Oh, God ! have mercy on my sire ! forgive the ' Cop-
  perhead !' "

I shudder at the thought, Jeff., of that dark, nether
  Hell.
Where you, and I, and all our clan, ere long will surely
  dwell ;
Fit subjects we shall be, Jeff., of that Infernal chief
Who first Rebellion's banner reared in Heaven's holy
  fielf.
Yes, 'midst that Demon crowd, Jeff., with hands of
  deepest red,
Scorned by the lesser damn'd, Jeff. shall live the
      " Copperhead !"

I'm going to make amends, Jeff., at least as best I can,
And cast the serpent's scaly pelt, and be again a man !
I mean to vote for Union men, Jeff., men of glorious
  fame,
Tried and trusty patriots, Jeff., I blush to hear their
  name.
Then, if a life of Truth, Jeff., can reconcile the past.
The victim of thy guile, Jeff., may sleep in peace at
  last.

SEYMOUR'S DREAM.

·RESPECTFULLY ADDRESSED TO ALL DEMOCRATS.

As Governor Seymour (may his tribe decrease)
Awoke one night, not very much at ease,
After a frightful dream, which made him stare,
And filled his soul with black despair,
He saw, beneath the shadow of his room,
An ugly phantom crouching in the gloom—
The Devil—writing fiercely in a book of brass,
That Seymour's riot-speech made of him an ass.
He to the shadow said (a little pale) :
"What scribest thou ? " The phantom raised his tail,
Then answered, with look of some discord :
" The names of those who own Jeff Davis Lord."
" Is mine one ? " said Seymour. " Not quite so,"
Replied the Devil. Seymour spoke more low,
Then said : " Pray, did again your pen,
And write me one who hates the Union men."
A pause ensued. The Devil looked more grave,
Then said to Seymour : " Dost thou hate the slave ? "
Said Seymour : " Yes, I hate to see them free,
For that will spoil our ' *Sham Democracy.*'
Pray, do me justice, Mr. Devil, do,
For since I've held my office I've been true,
To neighbor Jeff, and all his traitorous horde,
And hence I claim the right to call him Lord.
I've stood by him in every public act ;
None so base as to deny that fact.
I've never said a word in praise of Lincoln,
And hence have naught in that respect to think on.
Should the Abolition tribe this fact deny,
My Five Point friends can give them all the lie,
And ' Mackerelville ' can furnish quite a crew
To swear that I to Jeff, was always true."
The Devil switched his tail with glad delight,
Then wrote and vanished, but returned next night,
And showed the names who served Jeff. Davis best,
And lo ! H. Seymour's name led all the rest.

AMERICA MY AMERICA.

Air :——*Maryland, My Maryland.*

God of our native land to thee
       America, my America!
With swelling heart and bending knee,
       America, my America!
We offer thee our song of praise,
Our grateful tribute now we raise,
In sweeter strains and nobler lays,
       America, my America!
We bless thy name, Almighty God,
       America, my America!
For this fair land our fathers trod,
       America, my America!
This land we fondly call our own,
With countless blessings thickly strewn,
Our joy, our heritage, our crown,
       America, my America!
Here plenty reigns, here freedom sheds,
       America, my America!
Her choicest blessings on our heads,
       America, my America,
Here commerce spreads her ample store,
Which comes from every foreign shore,
Science and arts we here explore,
       America, my America!
These are gifts, Almighty King,
       America, my America!
From thee our matchless blessings spring,
       America, my America!
Our fruitful fields, our sunny skies,
Our liberty, our gospel joys,
All from thy boundless goodness rise
       America, my America!
With fearful war our land is pressed,
       America, my America!

But thou can'st send us peaceful rest,
        America, my America!
Do thou amidst our nation reign,
Here liberty and truth mantain,
And we will bless thy mighty name,
        America, my America!

THE LOYAL LEAGUER'S RESPONSE.

Suitable for any "Air."

A member of the "Union League," being asked
whether he was prepared to respond to the draft,
gave the following *patriotic* and characteristic answer:

        Yes,
Should our bleeding country ever need,
  My strong arm in her due defense,
Or require my heart's blood, indeed,
  And me to leave "sweet home," and, hence
To tread the bloody battle field,
  Where life is lost, but laurels won,
And for my "country's cause," to yield,
  All else of earth, it must be done
And self-prepared for any fate,
  Leave wife and home to Heaven's care,
I'll rush with loyal heart elate,
  And loyal love for country dear,
Nor grudging much the paltry sum,
  That saves from war all "snobs" and scholars,
And scoffing at conscription's drum
  I'll go, and save *three hundred dollars.*

A SOLDIERS SOLILOQUY.

A Legal Tender found its way into a Montgomery street-broker's office with the following soliloquy written legibly on its (green)back:

Oh, dear! what shall I do! for in this I beheld,
A substitute for silver, and a substitute for gold.
Of good my purse is empty, of victuals, stomach too.
With this substitute for silver, oh dear! what shall I
    do?
Shall I take it to a broker, and sell it for sixty-five,
For a little bit of silver, to keep this boy alive?
Or sell it for old rags, at thirty cents a per pound,
Then go and jump into the bay, and this poor mortal
    drown?
No, Sir! I'll buckle on my sword again, and go back to
    the wars.
And by the brave and glorious fighting, raise green-
    backs to the stars.

UNION COMING.

Say, bruders, hab you seen McClellan,
    Wid de sour look on his face.
Go down de road toward Salt Ribber,
    Like a man dat's run his race.
He heard a sound all too de country,
    Where the Union voters stay;
He says to Pen, we had better leab sudden,
    While we both can get away.
Chorus.—For Maine has said, Ha! ha!
      Vermont she say, Ho lio!
    We'll sing de song ob Union eber,
      From Maine to Mexico!

Mac may be smart, but Lincum's smarter,
    And de people tink so, too ;
And on de eight ob nex, November
    I can tell you what dey'll do.
Dey'll fix de flint ob all de traitors
    Who would hab us compromise,
And hoist de flag ob glorious Union
    Till it reaches to de skies.

De Copperheads dey feel so lonesome
    On de norf ob Dixie's line,
Dey all should move across de ribber,
    Whar Jeff Davis wants ter shine.
We're Abe and Andy and de Union,
    And do ole Flag tried and true ;
We don't tink we'll be confed-ra-ted
    By de rebel grayback crew

De doughface tries to help Jeff Davis,
    And he dodge around de stump ;
We'll put him yet where he'll hab to holler,
    Wid he head beneath de plump.
Their day is past, de word am spoken—
    In de Union all am free ;
We're good enough, smart enough, all to hab
    Union
    From de lakes to gulf and sea

WE WILL FIGHT IT OUT.

THE SOLDIERS OPINION OF THE CHICAGO PLATFORM.

AIR :—" *Whack rodwy Dow.*"

We have heard the rebels yell,
    We have heard the Union shout,
We have weighed the matter very well,
    And mean to fight it out ;

In victorys happy glow,
  In the gloom of utter rout,
We have pledged ourselves—" Come weal
    wo,
  By heaven ! we fight it out."

Chorus.—Whack rowdy dow
          How are you Chicago Platform,
        Whack rowdy dow
          How are you " Little Mac."

'Tis now too late to question
  What brought the war about ;
'Tis a thing of pride and passion,
  And we mean to fight it out.
Let the " big wigs" use the pen,
  Let them caucus, let them spout,
We are half a million weaponed men,
  And mean to fight it out.

Our dead, our loved, are crying
  From many a stormed redoubt,
In the swamps and trenches lying—
  " O, comrades fight it out!
'Twas our comfort as we fell
  To hear your gathering shout,
Rolling back the rebels' weaker yell—
  God speed you, fight it out ?"

The negro—free or slave—
  We care no pin about,
But for the flag our fathers gave
  We mean to fight it out ;
And while that banner brave
  One rebel rag shall flout,
With volleying arm and flashing glaive,
  By heaven ! we fight it out!

O, we've heard the rebel yell,
  We have heard the Union shout,
We have weighed the matter very well,
  And mean to.fight it out ;
In the flush of perfect triumph
  And the gloom of utter rout.
We have sworn on many a bloody field,
  " We mean to fight it out !"

SONG OF THE LOYAL SOLDIER.

AIR :—" *Jamie's on the Stormy Sea.*"

Comrades known in marches many,
  Comrades, tried in dangers many,
Comrades, bound by memories many,
    Brothers ever let us be,
Wounds or sickness may divide us.
Marching orders may divide us,
But whatever fate betide us,
    Brothers of the heart are we

Comrades, known by faith the clearest,
Tried when death was near and nearest
Bound we are by ties the dearest,
    Brothers evermore to be,
And, if spared, and growing older,
Shoulder still in line with shoulder,
And with hearts no thrill the colder,
    Brothers ever we shall be.

By communion of the banner,—
Crimson, white, and starry banner,—
By the baptism of the banner,
    Children of one Church are we,
Creed nor faction can divide us,
Race nor language can divide us,
Still whatever fate betide us,
    Children of the Flag are we!

NORTH MEN, TURN OUT.

AIR :—" *Burdhen herus .*"

Northmen, come out!
Forth unto battle with storm and shout!
Freedom calls you once again,
To flag and fort and tented plain ;
Then come with drum and trump and song,
And raise the war-cry wild and strong :
    Northmen, come out!

Northmen, come out!
The foe is waiting round about,
With paixhan, mortar, and petard,
To tender us their Beau-regard ;
With shot and sharpnell, grape and shell,
We give them back the fire of hell ;
    Northmen, come out!

Northmen, come out!
Give the pirates a roaring rout ;
Out in your strength and let them know
How Working Men to Work can go.
Out in your might and let them feel
How Mudsills strike when edged with steel,
    Northmen, come out!

Northmen, come out!
Come like your grandsires stern and stout ;
Though Cotton be of Kingly stock,
Yet royal heads may reach the block ;
The Puritan taught it once in pain,
His sons shall teach it once again ;
    Northmen, come out!

Northmen, come out!
Forth into battle with storm and shout!
He who lives with victory's blest,
He who dies gains peaceful rest.
Living or dying, let us be
Still vowed to God and Liberty,
    Northmen, come out!

WEIGHT FOR WEIGHT;

OR, GREENBACKS VS. GOLD.

Though roguish brokers daily try
  Our currency to mar,
In spite of them, Greenbacks and Gold
  Are sure to be at par.

For Chase and Abe both declare
  Our credit they'll uphold,
And make their thousand dollar notes
  Be worth their weight in gold.

UNCLE ABE.

AIR :—" *Nelly Bly.*"

Uncle Abe, Uncle Abe! here we are again!
We've got a platform now, we think, that will not
    bend or strain.
Beat the drum, unfurl the flag, Freedom is for all.
And so we fling it to the breeze as in the ranks we
    fall,
Chorus.—
    Ho Uncle Abe! Listen, Uncle Abe, and see!
    We sing for you, work for you, Hurrah for
      Liberty!

Uncle Abe we have tried, and we've found him true ;
We know that he is honest in the work he has to do.
Uncle Abe has his faults, and so have other men,
But in firmness for the Union we'll not find his like
 again.

Uncle Abe, Uncle Abe, never, never fail !
Never let the traitors back within the Union s pale ;
For Slavery made treason, and the   crime must
 punished be,
And the Constitution Platform shaped so all **men**
 shall be free.

Uncle Abe is the man for the work in hand ;
He knows the ropes about the ship upon whose
 deck we stand ;
Waves may dash and winds may roar, but he'll guide
 us on,
Till Secession's storm is o'er and the Port of Peace is
 won.

LINES TO A COPPERHEAD.

AIR :—" *Yet to be found.*"

You are a copperhead ! you loathsome creature,
 And seem to glory in your right to crawl ;
While treason stamped upon your every feature,
 Proclaims you serpent, venom, fangs and all.
The fetid filth and nauseous dust of party
 Serve you for daily food, and drink and slime ;
Just now you look robust, and hale, and hearty,
 Your snakeship must have had a high old time.

That was a pleasant dream of yours no doubt,
    And Copperheadom wagged its thousand tails,
At thoughts of leaving brave New England out,
    And fencing in the South and West with snakes for
        rails ;
But Davis, Toombs, your brother traitors, meet
    Your crawling sycophants with open scorn ;
With Northern traitors they're too proud to treat,
    Your Southern *brethren*, brethren " in a horn."

The rattle-snake, so shunned by old and young,
    Displays some honor when he goes to battle,
And ere he launches his envenomed tongue,
    Proclaims his presence by a warning rattle.
But you, vile copperhead, in silence working
    Your snaky folds along your slimy path,
And while he dreams no danger nigh is lurking,
    Strike the poor victim with your causeless wrath.

You great progenitor, as you have heard,
    With rank hypocrisy invaded Eden,
And with seductive smile and honied words,
    Beguiled old Eve to eat the fruit forbidden.
But like a gentleman he upright walked
    With graceful mien amid those bowers of bliss,
And with bland look and tone he smiling talked,
    While you from instinct only crawl and hiss.

Judas Iseariot when he sold his Savior,
    And had secured the promised bloody fee,
Was conscience-stricken at his vile behavior,
    And hung himself upon the nearest tree.
'Tis an example for your imitation,
    Go hang yourself! all honest men abhor you,
Or if you dread a suicide damnation,
    Just call on us, we'll find a halter for you.

You are a copperhead! On judgement day
    Most men are taught to fear, but you'll have two,—
The first when we return—oh! we'll repay
    In full the scorn of your vile reptile crew;
Then breathe one word of treason if you dare,-
    So bold, so brave, behind the soldier's back,
We'll leave your bones to dangle in the air,
    You crawling, slimy, sycophatic pack.

You are a copperhead! have read the story,
    ·How *our* sires wrought out *their* salvation,
Oh, there were traitors then, cow boy and tory,
    And you are but an heir to their damnation.
Their very names with infamy are rotten,
    As you will be when you return to dust;
Remembered but in scorn, if not forgotten,
    The synonym of loathing and disgust.

Back to your holes! Your breath is rank with trea-
        son,
    And honest men would like to walk abroad;
Out of our path! if only for a season,
    While Christian freemen breathe one prayer to
        God,—
A prayer that He would save our glorious Union
    From traitors that our homes and altars haunt;
Back! while our loyal sons hold high communion,
    In Freedom's name, vile copperhead, avaunt!

But stay one moment—you would seem to hold
    Toward the body politic two-fold relation;
You are the small-pox! shunned by young and old,—
    Just now your putrid virus taints the nation,
And for a season we can but endure you,
    Although enough the bravest to appall,
But Union remedies will quickly cure you,
    And leave nothing but a scab—that's all.

RALLY BOYS FOR UNCLE ABE.

Air :—" *We stand here United.*"

Now Rally, boys, rally! Now Unionist! rise!
With Lincoln and Johnson our foes we'll surprise;
The tempest may gather in madness and force,
Our good ship will hold to its true Union course.

Chorus.—For the right, for the right,
　　Here determined we stand,
　　So pledge we the word,
　　So join we the hand,
　　So pledge we the word,
　　So join we the hand.

Our Leader is with us, who four years ago,
Aloft held our banner; and to aim we know
The hearts of the people are bound by the ties
Of faith, and freedom. Arise, boys! arise.

From Rio Grande's waters, from Aristook's tide,
From Oregon's vallies, we'll gather in pride;
With shoulder to shoulder we'll march to the fight,
For Lincoln and Johnson, and Justice and Right.

Our cause is so Holy, our cause is so Just,
Our foes are such traitors, that conquer we must;
The banner of freedom must wave o'er the land;
Who stand on our soil as full freemen must stand,

By those who have fallen, by those who have
　died,
To pledge and to promise we'll surely abide;
Our ranks are not broken; with firm step we go,
And November shall herald defeat to the foe!

NEW NUSERY RHYMES.

Set to Nursery Airs.

Who comes here? Why, General G.
What do you want? The Presidency!
Where's your platform? Why, don't you see ?
Then get you gone, for it don't suit me!

    Mac and Pen, in town and glen,
      Put on their good behaviour;
    But Mac caved in, when he would win,
      And Pen could not find favor.

    General G. peace did not see!
      George P. did not like war!
    So, 'tween the two, what will they do?
      Why, sprawl upon the floor.

See-saw, sacradaw, sacradown,
Which is the way to Washington!
With one eye North and one eye South,
And double meaning in my mouth—
That is the way to Washington.

    Hey, diddle! diddle!
    The Platform's a fiddle,
With it I can play at the moon;
    Republicans scoff,
    But they can't push me off—
For I'm bound to reach Salt River soon.

ABE LINCOLN KNOWS THE ROPES.

AIR :—" *Any Tune.*"

Abram Lincoln knows the ropes !
All our hopes
   Centre now about the brave and true.
Let us help him as we can,
Abe's the man,
   Honest for the country through and thro ',

Others good, perhaps, as he
There may be ;
   Have we tried them in the war-time's flame ?
Do we know if they will stand,
Heart in hand,
   Seeking for the Right, in Heaven's name ?

Let the Nation ask him, then,
Once again
   To hold the rudder in the stormy sea ;
Tell him that each sleepless night,
Dark to light,
   Ushers in a morning for the Free.

Let us not forget our rude
Gratitude ;
   But lend our servant the poor crown we
     may ;
Give him four more years of toil,
Task and moil,
   Knowing God shall crown him in His day.

HOW WE LOVE THEIR SLAVERY.

Air :--" *Life on the Ocean Wave.*"

Are there any in our land,
Who with strong and fearless hand,
Dares to proudly, boldly stand
For the truth with bravery ?
Stand with face against the foe,
Deal him quickly blow for blow,
And the rebel traitors show
How we love their Slavery ?

Chorus.—Are there any &c, &c.,

Do we shrink from dangers front ?
Do we fear the battle's blunt ?
Do we fight with weapons blunt,
Gainst their force and knavery ?
Shall we tamely bend the head ?
Shall we—who have fought and bled—
Shall we have it of us said
That we loved their Slavery ?

No, we dare for truth to fight,
Plant the starry standard bright
North and South, and with its light
Drive away all Slavery ;
Fight the foe until he yield
Here at home, and in the field,
Till our banner stands revealed
Through the mist of Slavery.

THE SOUTHERN'S CALL;

OR NORTHERN COPPERHEADS.

Air :—"*Rally, snakes.*"

Come out, you slimy hussies,
Forget domestic musses,
And vend a few more cusses
   On Abolitionists.
      Wake, snakes !

Vallandigham will lead you,
While Southern traitors feed you ;
And oh, how bad we need you,
   'Gainst Abolitionists.
      Wake, snakes !

There's only one condition,
To save us from perdition
Just stop this Abolition !
   d——d Abolition!
      Wake, snakes !

There's nothing you can do, sirs,
To help both us and you, sirs,
Like making such ado, sirs,
   'Bout Abolition.
      Wake, snakes !

VOTE FOR LINCOLN.

Air :—"*O'er the Lake where droops the willow.*"

On the hill tops, fortress-crested,
   Long time ago,
Freedom's battles were contested,
   With a stern foe.

There the flag of Freedom flying,
　　Like Heaven's bow,
Nerved the living, cheered the dying,
　　Long time ago.

Sons of freemen, do the fires,
　　In your hearts glow,
That sustained your gallant sires
　　Long time ago?

Then arouse, a band of brothers!
　　To the world show,
Tyrant's chains may rest on others,
　　On you, never! no!

Vote for Lincoln, true and able,
　　And thus end the strife;
Be the voter white or sable,
　　'Tis the Nation's life.

———

WHO CRIES FOR PEACE

WHEN ALL IS WAR?

Peace, peace, peace, do you say?
　What! with the enemy's guns in our ears?
With the country's wrongs not rendered back?
　What! while the traitors stand at bay.
Hands dripping with blood, and the ocean bears
　The cursed flag on the merchantman's track?

Peace, peace, is still your word ?
  WE say you LIE, then!—that is plain.
There is no peace, and shall be none.
  Our very dead would cry "Absurd!"
And clamor that they died in vain,
  And strive to come back to the sun.

Hush! more reverence for the dead!
  They've done most for liberty
Evermore since the earth was fair,
  Or would that WE had died instead.
Still dreaming peace meant liberty,
  And did not, could not, mean despair.

Peace, you say? yes, peace in truth!
  But such a peace as tho car can achieve
'Twixt the rifle's crack and the rush of the ball.
  Not the tiger's spring and the crunch of the tooth,
Nor the ruthless traitor's negatitive,
  But God's peace—shining over all.

———

OUR SHIP OE STATE.

AIR :—"*Our Union right or wrong.*"

In the brave old days of " Eighty-Seven,"
  One heart—one hope—one fate,
We fashioned the model, and laid the keel,
  And builded our Ship of State ;
'Twas oak of our Northern mountains,
  And pine of our Southern hills,
And our Midland's cedar and iron,
  And our whole land's linking wills.

Britania ruled the waves then,
  Mistress of many a sea,
And the Red Cross flag was the signal,
  For the other flags to flee.

But over the broad Atlantic,
  As strong, as calm as fate,
Rode a gallant bark that fled from none,
  And that was our Ship of State.

Since the brave old days of Eighty-Seven,
  When we fashioned its glorious form,
And gave to the breeze its strips and stars,
  It has weathered many a storm.
But its captains have been of the truest men,
  And its crews of the bravest tars,
Adn though its foes have been mighty,
  It bears but a few faint scars.

With a continent to watch o'er,
  'Twas the bulwark of the Free,
With an ocean's path to open,
  'Twas the eagle of the sea.
It has won the world's applause,
  It has served the age's needs
Till it stands without a rival
  In the glory of its deeds.

From the brave old days of Eighty-Seven,
  'Till our evil days of late,
We've trusted the nation's safety
  With our gallant Ship of State ;
But now with a tempest gathering fast,
  And a sea that threats to whelm,
Her captain's craven and shrinking aghast,
  And fears to man the helm.

Oh, for a day of that vigor
  The nation knew of old,
When her flag had heroes and statesmen
  Beneath its every fold !
Oh, for an hour of manhood,
  To fix our wavering fate—
To bear on the helm with firmness,
  And rescue our Ship of State.

"FORWARD FOR LINCOLN AND THE UNION."

AIR :—"*March to the Battle Field.*"

'Tis a noble work for one's country to bleed,
To take up arms in its time of need,
Impelled by no selfish thought or greed
  Of ambition and power!
    To peril one's life
    In the deadliest strife
    That ever can curse,
    With its groaning hearse,
The land where freedom's bower
    Shows the rallying tree
    Of liberty.
Chorus.—'Tis a noble work, &c, &c.,

'Tis a noble work for one's country to bleed,
To respond to her call in her hour of need,
And wield the sword without thought or creed,
  Of ambition and power!
    To lead the van,
    Like a valiant man,
    Where wounds are crying,
    And patriots dying,
Neath an iron and leaden shower.
    Then forward to strike the foe
    Let our brave freemen go.

Far be the thought from those who think and feel ;
Far be it from men who can wield the steel!
Far be it from all who would not kneel
  Before their God as a coward!
    Down with the lying,
    Blasphemous, crying,
    Wicked shame
    Of rebellious flame,
And let the watch-word be forward!
    Forward to smite the foe
    Let our brave freemen go.

Was it invasions that stirred up the heart of the
   North?
Was it invasion that sent her grand armies forth?
If so, our cause were but little worth,
   And our children will weep
       O'er the desolation
       Of a mighty nation.
      'Tis the Haynes and Marions,
      Whose echoing clarions
Have burst from their keep,
    To rally us on,
    To sustain what their valor won.

Let us halt on our way—let us kneel by this grave,
And pray for the virtue that only can save
Our bark of state from the impending wave;
  Let us kneel at the tomb of Washington,
      For though the dead may not rise,
      He may hear us from the skies,
      And make his dying counsel heard
      His immortal farewell word—
Spoken ere he went death's journey on.
      One short prayer heavenward,
      And then march forward.

AMERICAN SLAVERY.

Air:—" *The Rock of Liberty.*"

Wipe out the blot! Wipe out the spot!
   Jehovah's sword is flaming high;
Wipe out the blot! Cut out the rot!
   In its own venom let it die!

It is the scorpion girt by fire;
   Self-kindled are the flames that spread;
In its own ire let it expire,
   Its own sting rankling in its head!

Wipe out the spot! Wipe out the blot!
   The parricidal, horrid thing;
For him be not a freeman's lot
   Who'd back to life the monster bring.

On to the long predestined end—
   The march of time is moving now!
As sweeps the surge events converge
   To rend the vail from freedom's brow.

Wipe out the spot! Wipe out the blot!
   The only stain our banners show;
O! who has not bewailed the lot
   That heap'd on us the bondman's throes!

We stand for all our country's law's;
   But now that they have rent the chain,
Who backward draws from Freedom's cause
   Let him not rank with men again!

The worm that eats the root is found;
   The surgeon's knife is at the sore;
Shall health abound? The tree grow sound,
   Or, conscious, wither as before?

It is for life! and ours the tale
   To sound to ages yet to come.
Shall fiends prevail? Shall Heaven fail?
   The answer leaps e'en from the dumb.

The cancer dries the vital flow
   While one polluting root remains;
And even so no healthful glow
   Can spread, where Slavery clogs the veins.

Behold the curse! Its desperate bands
 Are shaking now the sacred base,
Where Freedom stands with clenched hands
 And sinews stained to save her race.

Let no man fear! Our Eagle yet
 Will cleave the clouds that ride the wind,
Tho' Slav'ry fret, its star be set—
 His fight shall leave that night behind!

Still brighter smiles shall dress the soil
 Where sugar, rice, and cotton grow,
And freeman's toil shall know no foil,
 Though black or white his color show.

Wipe out the blot! Wipe out the spot!
 Jehovah's sword is flaming high!
Wipe out the blot! Cut out the rot!
 In its own venom let it die!

THE COPPERHEAD.

AIR :—" *The Rattle Snakes Hiss.*"

There's a venomous snake which lurks in the grass,
 A slimy, treacherous, horrible thing;
Of a copperish hue are his ugly folds,
 And he gives no warning before his sting,
 But strikes with a secret and sudden dart,
 Leaving a poisoned and deadly smart.

In the cool sweet meadows and over the fields,
 Mid the tall green shoots and the clover blooms,
He crawls along on his horrid scales,
 And through the depths of the forest glooms
 This hideous reptile his slow path takes,
 The vilest of all the race of snakes.

He basks in the light of the sun by day,
  And hides in his narrow den at night
Along with his mate and pestilent brood.
  Oh, a loathsome, hateful, repulsive sight
    Is this slimy serpent, this crawling thing,
    With the copperish hide and the deadly sting !

Of late he has taken the shape of man,
  As of old took Satan the serpent's form,
Plotting at night in his traitorous den,
  And lurking by day in the sunshine warm,
    Ready to strike with a secret dart
    His poisoned fangs to the Nation's heart.

More dangerous far than an open foe
  Is this cunning snake with fangs so keen,
Lying concealed in the tall green grass,
  And striving to hide his venomed spleen.
    Oh, what shall we do with the hateful thing
    To render harmless his poisoned sting ?

FATHER ABRAHAM WE ARE ARE COMING.

AIR:—*" We are Coming Father Abraham."*

Father Abraham ; coming are we now !
  From hill top and from glen,
And 'long the mountains shaggy brow
  Three hundred thousand men
Now march in the line once more,
  As erst they marched in days gone by
Along old ocean's rocky shore,
  With banners floating in the sky.

    We are marching on to battle
      And to the ballot-box.
    We shall bind our Union shouts,
      On a pile of Union Rocks.

Father Abraham ; coming are we now !
   As came the warriors of old time.
When shone their armor in the glow,
   Of sunlight of the Eastern clime.
Jerusalem in the hands of wicked men
   Speaks from her grottoes lone and drear,
And dusty squadrons crowd the plain,
   Whilst shouts of triumph strike the ear.

Father Abraham ; coming are we now !
   With horsemen like the crested main.
With hearts of oak and solemn vow
   To mingle 'mong the honored slain.
Our tents are pitched in valley's deep,
   And where the river's rushing stream,
Between the mountain's giant steep,
   Rolls 'neath the sun's red gleam.

Father Abraham ; coming are we now !
   From many a hall and humble cot,
Conspiracy's proud head to bow
   And trample on these *san culotties.*
Like rushing waves along the mead
   Our march is onward to the fight ;
Death in the van with whitened steed
   Leads on our hosts of Federal might.

Father Abraham ; coming are we now !
   The young with lightning in his eyes;
The old with snow locks on his brow,
   Starts the star banner to the sky.
Whilst the loud blast of the bugle-horn
   Rouses the warrior from his earthy bed,
And rushing to the fight at dewy morn

THE SOUTHERN MALBROOK.

Air :—— ' *Malborough o'er va-t-en guerre.*"

Jeff. Davis has gone to battle,
Tweedledum, tweedledum tweedledee ;
Jeff. Davis has gone to battle,
Nor knows when he'll return.

He'll return on the first of April,
Tweedledum, tweedledum, tweedledee ;
He'll return on the first of April,
Or on the Fourth of July.

But the Fourth of July is over,
Tweedledum, tweedledum, tweedledee ;
But the Fourth of July is over,
And Davis does not return.

Lady Davis calls her Congress,
Tweedledum, tweedledum, tweedledee ;
Lady Davis calls her Congress,
And mounts the Speaker's chair.

She there perceives her nigger,
Tweedledum, tweedledum, tweedledee;
She there perceives her nigger,
As black as the ace of spades.

" Nigger, my high-priced nigger,
Tweedledum, tweedledum, tweedledee ;
Nigger, my high-priced nigger,
What tidings do you bring ?"

" O Gorra, missis, de tidin's
Tweedledum, tweedledum, tweedledee ;
O Gorra, missis, de tidin's,
Dey'll make yer lily eyes weep.

" Took off yer summer muslin,
 Tweedledum, tweedledum, tweedledee
 Took off yer summer muslin,
 Also yer more anteek.

" Massa Jeff. is done gone dead,
 Tweedledum, tweedledum, tweedledee ;
 Massa Jeff. is done gone dead,
 Dead an' buried shu-ah !

" I seed him shove in de ground,
 Tweedledum, tweedledum, tweedledee ;
 I seed him shove in de ground
 By de Abolitioners !

" One follered wid his message,
 Tweedledum, tweedledum, tweedledee ;
 One follered wid his message,
 Anoder wid his letters ob Mark.

" One carried his dyin' 'fession,
 Tweedledum, tweedledum, tweedledee ;
 One carried his dyin' 'fession,
 Anoder some 'Federate bon's.

" Dey hung him on de gallus,
 Tweedledum, tweedledum, tweedledee ;
 Dey hung him on de gallus,
 Under de Stars an' Stripes.

" Around his tomb dey planted,
 Tweedledum, tweedledum, tweedledee ;
 Around his tomb dey planted
 De cussed Palmetter tree !

" Upon de topmost branches,
Tweedledum, tweedledum, tweedledee ;
Upon de topmost branches
De turkey buzzard sung.

" We seed his troubled spirit,
Tweedledum, tweedledum, tweedledee ;
We seed his troubled spirit
Fly ober de Cotton States.

" Secession fell to de ground,
Tweedledum, tweedledum, tweedledee ;
Secession fall to de ground,
Till it got up agin,

" To sing ob de victories,
Tweedledum, tweedledum, tweedledee ;
To sing ob de victories
Dat Massa Davis won.

" De sad occashun ober,
Tweedledum, tweedledum, tweedledee ;
De sad occasion ober,
De folks went home to bed."

TOGETHER—TOGETHER.

AIR :—" *Together !—Together !*"

ogether ! together ! Oh, why should we part ?
ogether in hand, and together in heart!
houlder to shoulder, as ever before,
h, still let us strive for the Union of yore !

Oh, well may we bleed as our forefathers bled,
For Liberty dies when the Union is dead.
Then still let us cling to our Union of old,
It is better than all of our lives and our gold.

Northerner, Southerner, still you are one,
Spite of the foul deed that traitors have done,
Spite of your bloodshed and spite of your hate,
Living or dead you are joined in your fate.

As one you have risen, as one you must fall!
And one flag or no flag must float over all.
For better or worse we have plighted our troth,
And the ruins of the Union must bury us both.

Then bloody and long though the contest may be,
Our freemen must fight for the cause of the free;
Though rivers of blood may yet deluge the land,
Our hearts must not fail us, nor slacken our hand.

No counting of cost ! for the Union is worth
All the lives of the South and the lives of the North.
For what is of value to you and to me,
If the stars shall be torn from the flag of the free?

Together ! together ! Join hands once again !
Though years be before us of toil and of pain.
Together ! together ! we conquer or fall,
For one flag or no flag must float over all !

SONG OF THE CROOKER.

AIR :—" *A Bullfrog sat on a Hickory Tree.*"

An old frog lived in a dismal swamp,
  In a dismal kind of way ;
And all that he did, whatever befell,
  Was to croak the livelong day.
    Croak, croak, croak,
    When darkness filled the air,
>   And croak, croak, croak,
    When skies were bright and fair.

" Good Master Frog, a battle is fought,
  And the foeman's power is broke,"
But he only turned a greener hue,
  And answered with a croak
    Croak, croak, croak,
    . When the clouds are dark and dun ;
    And croak, croak, croak,
    In the blaze of the noon-tide sun.

" Good Master Frog, the forces of Right
  Are driving the hosts of Wrong,"
But he gives his head an ominous shake
  And croaks out " *Nous verrons ?*"
    Croak, croak, croak,
    Till the heart is full of gloom,
    And croak, croak. croak,
    Till the world seems but a tomb.

To poison the cup of life
  By always dreading the worse,
Is to make of the earth a dungeon damp
  And the happiest life accursed.
    Croak, croak, croak,
    When the noontide sun rises high,
    And croak, croak, croak,
    Lest the night come bye and bye

TO GEORGE B. M'CLELLAN.

Air :—" *From the Battle Field.*"

Dear George, as you that fact discloses
That Grant is equal unto Moses
For cracking heads and breaking noses,
    And all such trifles ;
But Moses had not, I supposes,
    Such things as Rifles.

The *Flaming* hill, the Iron Thunder,
The Leaden Slret, if Jeff gets under
Such awful things, I should not wonder,
    If they don't shake him.
And if Grant does not make a blunder,
    He *p'raps* may take him.

But, if old Jeff should dare retreat,
  " The wild firey storms, the flash and beat,
In Iron Thunder and Leaden Sleet,"
    Will surely catch him,
And if they do not burn his feet
    Old Nick can't match him.

How smooth the verse, and how sublime,
They certainly will outlive old Time ;
It certainly would be a crime
    For to deny us
Some more when you can spare the time,
    As good and pious.

WHEN THIS WAR SO ENDED.

AIR:—"*Red, White and Blue.*"

When this war shall end in re-union
And we to our homes shall return,
With victory, peace, and sweet home—again
The heart of the patriot will burn.
While the loved ones at home wait to greet us,
Our duty all our thoughts should employ:
With the Star-Spangled Banner waving o'er
us—

Chorus,—Three cheers for the Union, boys,
Three cheers for the Union, boys,
With the Star-Spangled Banner waving
o'er us,
We'll cheer for the Union, boys.

THE OLD UNION WAGON.

AIR:—"*Wait for the Wagon.*"

In Uncle Sam's dominion, in eighteen sixty-one,
The fight between Secession and Union was begun:
The South declared they'd have the "rights" which
Uncle Sam denied,
Or in their secesh wagon they'd all take a ride.
Hurrah for the wagon, the old Union wagon!
We'll stick to our wagon and all take a ride!

The makers of our wagon were men of solid wit;
They made it out of "Charter Oak," that would not
rot or spilt;
Its wheels are of material the strongest and best,
And two are named the North and South and two the
East and West.

Our wagon-*bed* is strong enough for any "revolution,"
In fact, 'tis the " *hull*" of the " old Constitution,"
Her coupling's strong, her axle's long, and, anywhere
 you get her,
No monarch's frown can "back her down," no traitor
 can *upset* her.

This good old Union wagon the nation all admired ;
Her wheels had run for fourscore years and never
 once been " *tired;*"
Her passengers were happy, as along her way she
 whirl'd,
For the old Union wagon was the glory of the world.

But when old Abram took command, the South wheel
 got displeased ;
Because the *public fat* was gone that kept her axle
 greased ;
And when he gathered up the reins and started on
 his route,
She plunged into secession and knock'd some
 " felloes" out !

Now, while in this secession mire the wheel was
 sticking tightly,
Some tory passengers got mad and cursed the driver
 slightly ;
But Abram " couldn't see it," so he didn't heed their
 clatter :
" There's too much *black mud* on the wheel," says he :
 —" *that's what's the matter.*"

So Abram gave them notice that in eighteen sixty-
 three,
Unless the rebels " dried it up," he'd set their niggers
 free,
And then the man that led the van to fight against his
 nation
Would drop his gun, and *home* he'd run, to figh
 against *starvation.*

Around our Union wagon, with shoulders to the
    wheel,
A million soldiers rally, with hearts as true as steel ;
And of all the generals, high or low, that help to save
    the nation,
There's none that strikes a harder blow than *General*
    Emancipation !
    Hurrah for the wagon, the old Union wagon !
    We'll stick to our wagon and all take a ride !

WHAT ARE WE FIGHTING FOR.

AIR :—"*To be found in Richmond.*"

Note then the battle's din, and all the fierce array
Of war, the battle-smoke, the bloody fray,
Heart-touching moans, and piercing shrieks,
The dying groans and paling cheeks
Where death has stole the loved soul away ;
Where mangled forms that erst with life
And vigor strong, moved onward to strife,
Where beating hearts in brave men's breasts,
Beat stronger still through all the fiery tests
That mark on every side the awful day.
Dost ask what means this sad display,
Where death holds his court and feasts upon his prey
And riots fiercely in the wanton play ?

Dost ask, "What fight we for ?" Ask why
The thunder-cloud of time obscures the sky ;
Ask why the lightning flashes rend the air ;
Ask why the tempests rage that seem to bear
The fury of the demons as they fly ;
And Nature answers that the tempest's power
Was given it in Nature's quiet hour ;

The elements were brought together then,
Which in their rage and fury shake the abodes of men,
And in the dark'ning cloud that meets thine eye,
The purifying spirit dwells, whose angry glare
Is but the burning glance that purges from the air
The sick'ning, deathly vapors lurking there.

Thus in our country's quiet, when the smile of peace
Seemed wreathing all the land, and rich increase
Of wealth, and vast resources, led to power,
We nursed to life and vigor in that peaceful hour
The elements which now in war seek their release ;
And the tempests angry tumult is the sword.
Unsheathed by the Almighty, drawn to fulfil his
    word ;
We fight because God wills it—that our land may be
Indeed the *land of freedom,* when the oppressed are
    free
We profess to love our banner, may its glory never
    cease,
But we fight not for conquest, we fight not for fame,
But that the *Flag of Freedom* be worthy of its name ;
War is God's lightning glance, the purifying flame.

And when the storm shall pass, and sunlight fills the
    air,
'Twill disclose our starry banner still more beauteous
    and fair,
The same, the good old flag, each stripe and every
    star,
The symbols of our nation's glory, and afar
Its fame shall spread, and everywhere
Our banner, loved and honored over every land and
    sea,
Shall be esteemed with pride—*the Banner of the
    Free;*

And those who rally round it now, brave hearts, true
  as steel,
Firm and unflinching while the cannon's peal
And musket's roar the work of death declare,
Shall share in its new glory, when the foe
Which seeks the life of freedom, shall have felt the
  blow
Which breaks *forever* Slavery's chain, and lays the
  oppressor low.

LIGHT AND DARKNESS.

AIR :—" *The Inauguration.*"

O, God ! our way through darkness leads,
  But Thine is living light ;
Teach us to feel that Day succeeds
  To each slow-wearing Night ;
Make us to know, though Pain and woe
  Beset our mortal lives,
That Ill at last in death lies low,
  And only Good survives.

Too long th' oppressor's iron heel
  The saintly brow has pressed ;
Too oft the tyrant's murd'rous steel
  Has pierced the guiltless breast ;
Yet in our souls the seed shall lie,
  Till Thou shall bid it thrive,
O, steadfast faith that Wrong shall die.
  And only Right survive.

We walk in shadow ; thickest walls
  Do man from man divide ;
Our brothers spurn our tenderest calls,
  Our holiest aims deride ;

Yet though fell Craft, who fiendish thought
    Its subtle web contrives,
Still falsehood's textures shrink to naught
    And only truth survives.

Wrath's clouds our sky ; War lifts on high
    His flag of crimson stain ;
Each monstrous birth o'erspreads the earth
    In battles glory stain ;
Yet still we trust in God the Just,
    Still keep our faith alive,
That, 'neath Thine eye, all Hate shall die,
    And only love survive.

"AM I FOR PEACE—YES!"

Air :—*As Found in every Union Heart.*

For the peace which rings out from the cannon's
    throat,
And the suasion of shot and shell,
Till rebellion's spirit is trampled down
    To the depths of its kindred hell.

For the peace which follow the squadron's tramp,
    Where the brazen trumpets bray
And drunk with the fury of storm and strife,
    The blood red chargers neigh.

For the peace that shall wash out the leprous stain
    Of our slavery----foul and grim—
And shall sunder the fetters which creak and clank
    On the down-trodden black man's limb.

I will curse as traitor, and false of heart,
  Who would shrink from the conflict now,
And will stamp it with blistering burning brand,
  On hideous Cain-like brow.

Out! out of the way! with your spurious peace,
  Which would make us rebellion's slaves;
We will rescue our land from the traitorous grasp,
  Or cover it over with graves.

Out! out of the way! with your knavish schemes,
  You trembling and trading pack!
Crouch away in the dark like a sneaking hound,
  That its master had beaten back.

You would barter the fruit of our father's blood,
  And sell out the Stripes and Stars,
To purchase a place with rebellion's votes,
  Or escape from rebellion's scars.

By the widow's wail, by the mother's tears,
  By the orphans who cry for bread,
By our sons who fell, we will never yield,
  Till rebellion's soul is dead!

300,000 MORE.

We are coming Father Abraham, three hundred thou-
  sand more,
From Mississippi's winding stream, and from New
  England's shore;
We leave our plows and workshops, our wives and
  children dear,
With hearts too full for utterance, three hundred
  thousand more.

We dare not look behind us but steadfastly before ;
We are coming, Father Abram, three hundred thousand more.

If you look across the hill-tops that meet the Northern sky,
Long moving lines of rising dust your vision may descry ;
And now the wind, an instant, tears the cloudy vail aside,
And floats aloft our spangled flag in glory and in pride.

And bayonets in the sunlight gleam, and bands brave music pour,
We are coming, Father Abram, three hundred thousand more.

If you look all up our valleys, where the growing harvests shine,
You may see our sturdy farmer-boys fast forming into line ;
And children from their mother's knees are pulling at the weeds,
And learning how to reap and sow, against their country's needs.

And a farewell group stands weeping at every cottage door,
We are coming, Father Abram, three hundred thousand more.

THE END.

www.ingramcontent.com/pod-product-compliance
Lightning Source LLC
Chambersburg PA
CBHW022032080426
42733CB00007B/811